A Book of Small Poems Illustrated with Images

HEARTSCAPES

VOLUME 1

D1825326

JAYANT

INDIA · SINGAPORE · MALAYSIA

Notion Press

Old No. 38, New No. 6
McNichols Road, Chetpet
Chennai - 600 031

First Published by Notion Press 2019
Copyright © Advait Jayant 2019
All Rights Reserved.

ISBN 978-1-64733-902-9

"And think naught you can direct the course of love, for love, if it finds you worthy, directs your course."

– Khalil Gibran

My dear, You know? you have no escape.
You are imprisoned forever in my

Scape!

Remnant of our love…
Is my being's essence,
Is summing up of my life,
On earth, my presence!

I put some scattered words together
And claim to possess, instinct creative;
My Lord, forgive me for this arrogance,
It is your world, your words and narrative!

Creator, after creating me, you abandoned me in your moving creation!
Was it to get lost into the maze of affairs, or asking me to seek my origin, end?
Why did you programme such a complex game of rebirth and liberation?
Was it to watch me confused, or struggling to read secret messages you send!

Do all tiny little particles know what wind does to them?
It blows them somewhere, sometimes lets them rest;
Do my thoughts, my actions really matter, my Lord?
I walk, holding your hand, and think that it is my quest!

I walk on the thin line of life and death;
And yet live as if I am never going to die;
What if I die, shall I be born on the earth
Or become a tiny part of the infinite sky?

In your dreamy eyes,
is there my thoughts' little shade?
Are you letting weave in your long hair,
 my dream a thread?
If you say yes, I won't believe;
don't say No, I am afraid;
Let me get used to sleepless nights,
 let your silence invade!

Should I thank God for
giving me a heart
which is able to love,

Or to you, my dear,
who gave birth to that
intense emotion?

Oh, why do I trouble myself
by combining or
juxtaposing the two?

Let me bow down
to the Creator and to you
his wonderful creation!

As all the thoughts leave me one after the other,
I stand naked alone in the universe so dark;
To me it gives purpose; to my life, meaning;
From a distance as I see you like a bright spark!

God gave me another day to dream of you and think of you,
Thousands of thoughts, glorious past and future that shines,
That is how I have been sailing through all troubled waters,
As my offering to the Almighty, in your praise, I write four lines!

Images I create
by pouring colours on canvas;

You missed the point
that its source was inside;

You enquired about
paints, brushes, and techniques;

I wish you had thought of
inspiration behind!

Each stroke of brush soaked in emotions,
Is a line of poetry written in your praise;
It is your stories and images captured in stillness,
It is just a reflection of feelings that you raise!

Are you a divine melody that turned into a beauty
Or a beautiful being turning self into music?
Your twinkling eyes send stars to the universe,
Or you live on the earth, inviting energy cosmic!

Travelling on the never-ending road of love,
Few flowers but many thorns, what a strife!
The heart has to throb; ache and break, and
Gather itself again, what's otherwise life!

Your memories in my heart, take the form of a sea,
Each thought of you then rises like high tide;
Strange it is so that I feel blessed anyway;
When I drown deep in or the waves when I ride!

I open my eyes
life takes the driving wheel;
As I close them,
along with me you walk;
I speak to show the world
that I, too, exist.
When I am quiet,
it is just you and me talk!

My heart may be made of stone,
Your glance is no less than a hammer;
You chisel it in different shapes,
And script my love's grammar!

Let my mind get invaded
by your thoughts;
Let my emotions
travel through my body wild;
You are my sun and moon,
my earth and universe.
I am your father, brother,
lover, and child!

So many people, places and travel;
Life through chaotic lanes slow and fast;
The current of time drags me nowhere
Just by your thoughts with me, I am never lost!

In my empty heart
of inverted bowl of sky*,
Birds of your thoughts
fly night and day;
I capture those transiting
shapes and forms,
In my paintings, thus,
you live, sing, and sway!

*Inspiration – Omar Khayyam

As you sang on the stage and made the hall divine,
My heart kept melting with each line of the song;
The light and fragrance are not from scented candles,
It's my molten heart at your door in the night long!

A million stars in the sky;
I join to sketch your face;
You smile from there, the earth,
Moves with little more grace!

In your heart when you name my whisper,
It floats through the mountains on the air;
It intoxicates my mood, freshens up my skin,
Sparkles my heart and makes me younger!

They say you do good, better will follow;
They say you do bad, worse will follow;
Let me love you my dear day and night—
Let the love grow, and bliss will follow!

For me the sky is never an empty space;
I don't mean stars or planets or galaxy's atlas,
Or the clouds those float through the day;
It's your images that I draw on that canvas!

From your body when the morning breeze flows;
It brings through the mountains your fragrance;
All the buds in my small garden, assimilate it,
When they blossom, blossom with more elegance!

In the hectic mass of daily flow of work;
I see you floating on my heartscape;
It saves me from getting drowned in it.
With you, I float, all chaos I escape!

Like everyone I too fell in love;
Love must have huge gravity?
Later all the rules stand on their heads.
Days full of dreams, what's reality?

My fingers through your hair
added a few couplets;
To the song which
your lips had written on my body;
Our melted hearts together
will take it to a crescendo;
Let us share it with the world,
as it is of everybody!

Our song will be on their lips;
We don't have to write it on the walls;
It has discoveries of a rising Sun;
It has mysteries of a star that falls!

I surrender myself to the arms of the night;
Closing my eyes hope to see a new day;
To withstand nightmares, day's trauma;
For the glimpses of your smile, I pray!

A tinge of the fragrance of your hair;
The morning sea breezes bring;
I walk through the day half–drunken;
Like the owner of the world moving!

Some melted through your glances;
Some I tore between us those covers;
So many mysteries we thus uncovered;
By being one and becoming lovers!

Lips on Lips and your hair on my shoulder;
Your hands around me like wings of a swan;
That warmth has made my life so festive;
From dawn to the dusk and dusk to dawn!

Every day you are fresh like a flower;
As if soaked in a rose-jasmine shower;
Let me fill myself, with that fragrance;
Let my words be perfumed by its power!

why should I have control over heart's passion? which has taken over my body, mind & soul

I had to tear open my
well-guarded heart;
To make you my
infinite universe's part;
As you healed the wounds
by being inside;
I became a prisoner,
and now you, rule my heart!

I didn't want to become a poet or a painter;
I don't aspire to become divine or a monster;
Let me be your friend, your man, and lover;
Let that make me whatever—saint or sinner!

I never thought my broken
heart is capable of love,
You came into my life and
brought all pieces together,

I don't know what is
the shape of my heart today;
But now it beats for you,
day and night and forever!

Each particle in my body is in a mood to revolt;
Each with a thousand eyes longs for your glimpses;
Each with a thousand lips wants to pick up honey from you;
Each holding its own heart, waits for the caresses!

I feel the excitement when you are around;
The fragrance of your body plays that trick;
Away from you, I am lonely and cold;
Believe me or not, I turn into an ascetic!

It's raining so heavily today,
Right in front of me, I can't see
Memories come like a shower,
The world becomes just you and me!

Later...
These drops when rolling on my body
They soul my perfume and nurture.
Past feelings stir, blurs my present
Heart takes a flight to a fresh future!

Let me brush your hair by my fingers,
Dress you with finest emotions very light,
Let me paint your lips by my eyelashes and;
You be the most beautiful woman tonight!

Mature let our love like
red white rose sweet wine,

In the barrel of raw wood
of emotions let it settle down;

Let us not bottle it up
to sip and forget in a while,

Let us swim in it forever,
let us drink and in it drown!

You linger in me, whenever we part,
you caress my soul and kiss my heart,
You remain in me, even when away,
Nights I think of you and day my start!

Why such moments in my life are so few?
I pick up from your lips some drops of dew!
Your eyes oceans blue, do not give any clue,
I breathe from your soul, life becomes new!

Sometimes I become wild,
Like a mischievous child,
Try to hold your hand,
For you to be my guide!

With your lips, you kiss my words,
They will turn into a beautiful song;
I shall remain here or not dear,
They will be with you all along!

Those in love tomorrow may think
Their feelings are not new but old
As I know, yours are with me from ages
Which made me wild and bold!

These songs of me and you,
These songs are for him and her,
These whispers from heart to heart,
Will wander among lovers forever!

If my words could bring a little warm golden shower,
Creator, I pray you bless each day of mine with a line;
I gather rolling drops from her lovely body;
And drink them like nectar, honey, and sweet wine!

Your eyes for me are as rising and setting sun,
As you raise your glance, fly a thousand birds;
With their flights, they write poems on the sky,
For singing in your praise, I use their words!

You splash from your eyes the ink on the sky,
You kiss the sun and set it to crimson flame,
You swing your hair and earth starts moving,
For my world's chaos or rhythm, you are to blame!

Sharing each other's fantasies, when we played that game,
I was always surprised why you used to like all of them,
It was enough for you as long as you and I were together,
In bliss, only I should be; others for you were all the same!

Sometimes so lovely like day bright,
Sometimes so cold like a dark night,
You said you are always on the move,
I should check if my perspective is right!

Whether I am in bliss or head in a spin,
I walk along the line of love very thin,
Thus I feel you in all times and seasons,
It's not a game I play to lose or win!

I saw you, and you set the fire
deep in my heart,

For you are the spark
and you light the flame,

It burns into ash or
turns into gold, you said,

"It's up to your elements,
for love is that game!"

I always wondered
how you could instantly,

Taking a sip of wine
send it to each body part;

I saw it in your eyes
and tasted it from your lips,

Later, to realize
the source was your heart!

To turn over from
your book of romance,

I am not a few lines
or just a page;

I am the novel,
the beginning and its end,

I am the hero and villain,
the greedy, and the sage!

61

You walk through the day,
the way you wish,

I pray you keep,
a little time for me free,

For my emotions to drib
down to your roots,

Not to remain just on
a branch of your tree!

We cannot be normal friends,
We are extra-ordinary partners;
We are not made for the world,
We are just passionate lovers!

Lady listen, I am not your gentleman,
You are my woman, and I am your lover;
Through my heart, you race my blood,
Each time you hold me, I become younger!

Stitch them or glue them,
All the pieces of my heart,
I am in love with you totally,
Not part-time or in part!

When you and I
create a new universe of love,

No sacrifice will be required
on society's altars,

It will change in that moment
geometry of stars,

All planets will bless,
including Saturn and mars!

Your love showered seeds and brought rain,
Of hope and dreams in my heart's land barren,
Your fragrance inspired my days and nights,
As my heart has turned into a lovely garden!

Strings of your thoughts
vibrate in my body,

I live in its orchestra,
every night and day,

I thank the heavens
for giving this time in life,

They turn into a song,
when a few words I say!

When you dance for me, my dear,
for your steps – don't follow my heart;
It has a habit of beating unevenly,
'They' will laugh then at your art!

But if you dance on my heartbeat,
It may have its lovely charms,
As you lose your rhythm and balance,
You will fall surely in my arms!

In those deep loving songs
which with me you share,

Or the fragrance of your body
that floats in the air,

I am immersed in the waves
 you create around me,

Where joy meets with sorrow
and hope with despair!

Earlier it was only my heart, now its also home,
which is filled with your thoughts, feelings, and charm,
I let them flow from room to room, floor to floor,
they heal   wounds of years with their touches warm!

Precious has always been for me, at me, each your glance,
I wait for you to take just one step and ten steps I advance,
When you sing your songs for me, they take me into a trance,
Moon and stars conspire with me for you to become my best chance.

Take a sip from my
glass of wine,
And make its
every drop divine,
I let them drip into
my soul slowly,
Then beats will be yours
in the heart of mine!

Your lips hum
melody from heaven,
As our hearts set
the rhythm for the night,
My fingers search
chords on your body,
As our souls meet,
floats music light!

I am drowning in the stream of sorrow,
Shall I get up in the morning tomorrow?
I want to dream of her a day more;
Lord Can I one more day from you borrow!

I am neither a writer
nor a poet;
I don't understand
wordplay;
A spark, however,
lightened inner self,
Is burning within
my heart of clay!

Pour whatever,
to extinguish it;
Hardened, vulnerable
heart has become;
You hurt it,
 it cracks and collapses,
Each piece tells a story,
recites a poem!

How much sorrow can wine drain?
Lot of it slowly dribs into my heart,
Not these lines, paintings or music,
Smile while living in pain is art!

If your love was true,
why now total indifference?
If my feelings were a mask,
why only I am in pain?
How do I reconcile
these contradictions in my life,
Let me bury my heart
deep inside my brain!

If I am born again, let me be born as a man
Let my heart suffer in cycles of joy and sorrow;
Liberation promises bliss, monotonous, will it not be?
If heart breaks today, I wait for my love tomorrow!

Like balloons, burst,
in the rising ball of a dream,
I fall flat on face,
hurt and hit by the reality;
There are pieces of dreams
scattered everywhere;
I find in them love and life;
madness and sanity!

Tears kept on dropping from eyes,
Blue turned into crimson skies;
Earth tremored to give me shelter;
As I chose love over being wise!

You said many times,
my poems are precious,
You will keep them always
close to your heart;
In a click, they vanished...
from your heart's screen,
Into meaningless words,
they are broken apart!

I don't want to fight with you till your last move,
Win and be lonely king in the game of chess,
Ask your lost pawns not to throw stones at me,
I am not the one who bleeds yet can bless!

When the dust within settles down in the evening,
And I am left with only my empty inner space;
Each atom begins bringing your memories to life,
And create a storm in my heart till morning rays!

So you began your search for a heart?
Who would love you day night forever!
After taking a trip around the earth,
You reached, I was standing where!

I don't know how many months are left,
maybe a couple of years;
I don't want to spend longing for you,
with my eyes full of tears;
You have undone the delicately woven
 together our nest of love;
Gifting me eternal pain,
liberated me from daily anxieties and fears!

Because you felt my love in phases,
You thought my love was in transience;
You did not realize the context of changing it,
Thus missed eternal source's brilliance!

You treat me like
just a drop of rain,
You treat me like
only a flake of snow,
Yet I fill my whole world
with your colours,
Paint on my heart's sky
you as a rainbow!

My heart will hold on to your thoughts,
Even when you keep ignoring it,
Let it break with love and pain,
Rather than emptiness ruining it!

Are you really beginning a new life, that too with a bang?
Are you forgetting all the songs that together we sang?
How can we stop visiting the fantasies which we had created,
Let us pray that they shall come to us like a boomerang!

As I go out of your focus, my world turns into darkness;
With your glance at me, it comes back to existence;
As you know this watching my up downing madness;
You put me daily through life and death's experience!

You let my love slowly go away,
In different ways, you started to show,
It may pierce into another's heart,
Arrow of love—mine, blame—your bow!

You are not in my front that I could read your body language;
I cant see the dance of your brows and your answering gaze;
The days are gone when the silence was love's language;
My words now shall chase you, catch you, tease you and amaze!

Tomorrow when
you walk away from me;
I am not going
to chase your dream;
I shall live with
your memories in the heart.
Let them whisper, speak,
sing, and scream!

The question is not when you go away,
In my heart, who shall take that place;
The question is whether it can hold someone,
And shall it accept the new face?
Would it accept a new face, I doubt,
Sure it is not going to beat the same way,
How long will it continue to beat –
That the question, dear, when you go away!

All our lively conversations
Are on my fingertips;
Like prayers in my heart and
Songs on my lips!
Let us remain in silence,
Not disturb them,
Watch the blessed teardrop that
From wall of heart dribs!

To hide the bruises and rashes,
I burnt my heart into ashes;
Cover my mind's mirror with it;
Whenever your image in it flashes!

You pushed me into the dark,
Hoping that star of love on you shine;
While love supports no laws, it has
Its own maths divine!
It will make you understand
What it means to break a heart,
Easier to express in each situation,
For in my poems, you will find a line!

End? No! Let us again start;
I put at your feet my golden heart;
This is my offering and prayers;
Bless me, say Amen, on your part!

Is it not you who is in the light of my eyes?
Is it not you who mirrors in my heart?
Is it not you who perfumes my soul?
If it is true, then why should we part?

Just because I have some
physical comforts around me;
They think that my sorrow
is artificial and life is a theatre;
Sad that you too misjudged
my love as an Act of a play;
And crushed my heart,
not waiting for the drama to be over!

What if you are
surrounded by
hundreds of people,
I too of
your thoughts
create in my heart
a crowd;

What if you
sing and dance
with them often;
Alone,
but not lonely,
of my company,
I too am proud!

What if in the night
in my bed I keep turning;
What if I do not get up
with you in the morning;
Is it not a blessing that
you remain a part of me;
And the flame of our love
is still in me burning!

Memories of you
pour like heavy rain,
Through the million
cracks into my heart;
They are adhesive,
and they only strike
They keep it whole
and separate each part!

I started cutting the branches of love from my tree of life,
I stopped watering the plant of love and thought it would die;
But you created a garden in me of trees, creepers, and flowers;
Plant of love, tree of life, can't be distinguished by the naked eye!

When we cross each other,
why don't you stop for a while,
Please don't give that cold stare
at least fake me a smile,
Your indifference has changed
meanings for my life dear,
Once master of your heart has now
become a slave in exile!

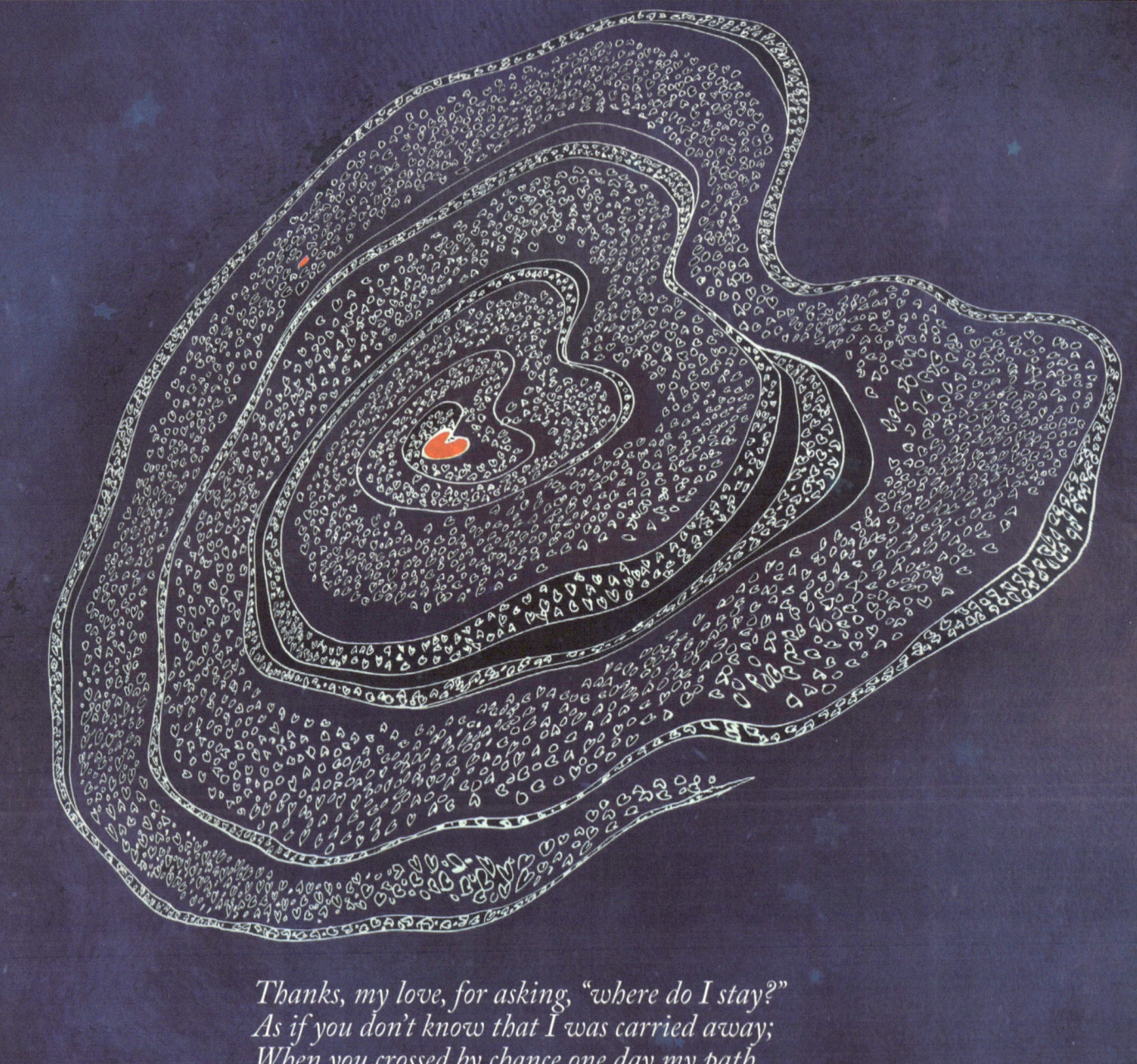

Thanks, my love, for asking, "where do I stay?"
As if you don't know that I was carried away;
When you crossed by chance one day my path
Since then I am lost somewhere in the milky way!

I hammered a nail in the wall,
To hang your portrait, I drew;
So that chaos in the studio's heart,
Pieces of my scattered life you view!

As I struggle to pick up the colours,
It's so strange that you keep changing;
You suffer my sorrows, you live joys,
From the wall of my heart, my darling!

They showed me paintings and sculptures,
Of Goddesses—ancient, Greek, and Roman,
They may be beautiful even ideal and perfect,
For me, you are the definition of a woman!

Good that you broke
my heart into a thousand pieces)
It turned out to be a bliss
rather than a curse,
When I remember good times
they gather into a painting,
When remembering how you hurt me,
they turn into a verse!

Sane, I tell myself, I should think always,
Before I get wild, crazy, nasty and unkind,
I wish I had control over my heart's passion,
Which takes over my body, soul, and mind!

I know this fire will destroy me one day,
But that gives me purpose and let me live,
Let me suffer, I ensure that you will not,
This is the game I play my love to survive!

The thought to meet you
after decades few,
Shortened my night
and made morning brighter,
Yet palms became moist,
heart sank worrying,
Would its broken pieces
become now even sharper?

The pieces did move, within,
although gently,
Like an orchestra
making divine music,
I looked within later
and was happy to see,
They were arranged
into a beautiful mosaic!

When you realized that I cannot fit in your world small,
You abandoned me from peak ensuring my deep fall,
You thought thereafter I will be limping or even crawl,
But no... I found strong wings, and now I fly very tall!

I know that I am just an atom in the vastness of Your Universe,
But that gave me an imagination that I could be one with thee,
I don't feel like a dust particle being carried away by the wind,
I am the wind together with this earth, fire, sky, and the sea!

Remnant of our love
is not only pain,
It's also imprints
of kisses on my heart,
Ancient engravings
on my soul and body,
My being, it turned
into a museum of art!

CPSIA information can be obtained
at www.ICGtesting.com
Printed in the USA
LVHW072055200120
644167LV00002B/8

9 781647 339029